2010

BIG STARS BIG PICTURES

SPORTS ILLUSTRATED KIDS BOOKS

Managing Editor Bob Der
Creative Director Beth Power Bugler
Assistant Managing Editor Justin Tejada
Project Editor Andrea Woo
Assistant Photo Editor Gina Houseman
Writers Tommy Craggs, Luke O'Brien

TIME INC. HOME ENTERTAINMENT

Publisher Richard Fraiman
General Manager Steven Sandonato
Executive Director, Marketing Services Carol Pittard
Director, Retail & Special Sales Tom Mifsud
Director, New Product Development Peter Harper
Assistant Director, Bookazine Marketing Laura Adam
Assistant Publishing Director, Brand Marketing Joy Butts
Associate Counsel Helen Wan
Brand & Licensing Manager Alexandra Bliss
Design & Prepress Manager Anne-Michelle Gallero
Book Production Manager Susan Chodakiewicz
Associate Brand Manager Allison Parker

Special Thanks: Christine Austin, Glenn Buonocore, Jim Childs, Rose Cirrincione, Jacqueline Fitzgerald, Lauren Hall, Jennifer Jacobs, Suzanne Janso, Brynn Joyce, Mona Li, Robert Marasco, Amy Migliaccio, Brooke Reger, Dave Rozzelle, Ilene Schreider, Adriana Tierno, Alex Voznesenskiy, Sydney Webber

Copyright © 2010 Time Inc. Home Entertainment

Published by Time Inc. Home Entertainment

Time Inc.
1271 Avenue of the Americas
New York, New York 10020

ISBN 10: 1-60320-831-3
ISBN 13: 978-1-60320-831-4

Sports Illustrated Kids is a trademark of Time Inc.

We welcome your comments and suggestions about
Sports Illustrated Kids Books. Please write to us at:
Sports Illustrated Kids Books
Attention: Book Editors
PO Box 11016
Des Moines, IA 50336-1016

If you would like to order any of our hardcover Collector's Edition books, please call us at 1-800-327-6388.
(Monday through Friday, 7:00 a.m.— 8:00 p.m. or Saturday,
7:00 a.m.— 6:00 p.m. Central Time).

PHOTO CREDITS

Front Cover: Walter Iooss Jr. (James); David Bergman (Brady); Chuck Solomon (Pujols)

Back Cover: Al Tielemans (Peterson, Utley); Bob Rosato (Howard)

Page 3: David Bergman (Brady); David E. Klutho (Lincecum, Crosby); Greg Nelson (Howard); John Biever (Pujols, Manning, Peterson); Damian Strohmeyer (James); Al Tielemans (Utley); Simon Bruty (Brees); Jed Jacobsohn/Getty Images (White)
Pages 4–7: Bob Rosato (Brady portrait);
John Biever (Brady action)
Pages 8–11: Mike Powell (Lincecum portrait);
Brad Mangin (Lincecum action)
Pages 12–15: Walter Iooss Jr. (Howard portrait);
John W. McDonough (Howard action)
Pages 16–19: Howard Schatz (Pujols portrait);
Chuck Solomon (Pujols action)
Pages 20–23: Bill Frakes (Manning portrait);
John Biever (Manning action)
Pages 24–27: Heinz Kluetmeier (Crosby portrait);
Lou Capozzola (Crosby action)
Pages 28–31: Walter Iooss Jr. (James portrait);
Greg Nelson (James action)
Pages 32–35: John W. McDonough (Peterson portrait);
Fred Vuich (Peterson action)
Pages 36–39: Al Tielemans (Utley portrait);
Chuck Solomon (Utley action)
Pages 40–43: Al Tielemans (Brees portrait);
Damian Strohmeyer (Brees action)
Pages 44–47: Cameron Spencer/Getty Images (White portrait); Marc Piscotty/Icon SMI (White action)
Page 48: David E. Klutho (NHL Winter Classic);
Mickey Pfleger (Marino); Mike Powell (Lincecum);
Jamie Squire/ALLSPORT (Manning);
Damian Strohmeyer (James)

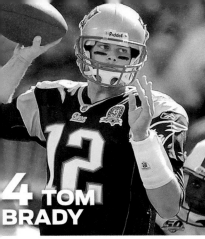

4 TOM BRADY

8 TIM LINCECUM

BIG STARS BIG PICTURES

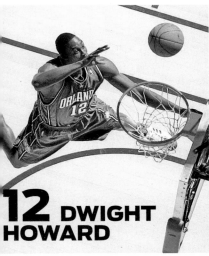

12 DWIGHT HOWARD

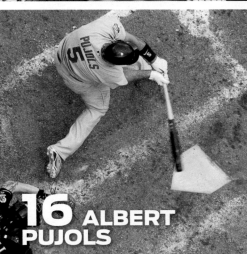

16 ALBERT PUJOLS

20 PEYTON MANNING

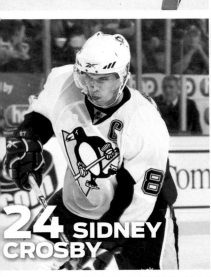

24 SIDNEY CROSBY

28 LeBRON JAMES

32 ADRIAN PETERSON

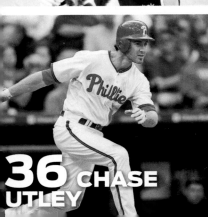

36 CHASE UTLEY

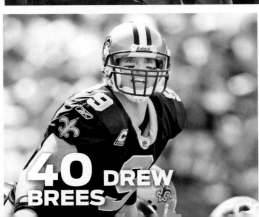

40 DREW BREES

44 SHAUN WHITE

RISING TO THE TOP

He's the face of the NFL, the golden boy with the golden arm. But Tom Brady's road to greatness had a few potholes. Brady was seventh on the depth chart in college at Michigan until he battled his way into the starting lineup his junior year. As a senior, he led his team to a dramatic overtime win in the Orange Bowl.

Life didn't get easier in the NFL. Drafted with the 199th pick in the sixth round by the New England Patriots in 2000, Brady completed only one pass for six yards his rookie season. It was only after starting quarterback Drew Bledsoe was injured in '01 that Brady got his shot. He didn't waste the opportunity. By the end of that season, Brady had expertly guided the Patriots to their first Super Bowl victory.

Brady led New England to two more Super Bowl titles over the next three seasons and evolved from an efficient game manager into an offensive powerhouse. With the additions of receivers Randy Moss and Wes Welker, Brady lit up the league in 2007. He set the single-season record for touchdown passes (50) and led the Pats to an undefeated regular season and yet another trip to the Super Bowl. Although New England lost to the New York Giants in a thriller, 17–14, Brady's place among the all-time greats was secure.

A knee injury in the season-opening game erased Brady's hopes of avenging the Super Bowl loss. But his return to form in 2009 proved that Brady — with toughness to match his talent — will continue to be one of the NFL's most dominant quarterbacks.

BIG NUMBERS

50
Touchdown passes that Brady threw in 2007, a single-season NFL record.

100
Passes completed by Brady in his four Super Bowl appearances. No other quarterback has connected on more throws than Brady in the big game.

21
Consecutive regular season wins by the Patriots from 2006 to '08. (Brady started 20 of those games.) It is the longest winning streak by a team in NFL history.

HE SAID IT

" I want to play until I'm 41. And if I get to that point and still feel good, I'll keep playing. I mean, what else am I going to do? I don't like anything else."

BIG MOMENTS

» Brady won the MVP award in 2007. He guided the Patriots to an undefeated regular season by throwing for 4,806 yards, the third-highest passing total of all time.

» Brady was named Super Bowl MVP in 2002 after throwing for 145 yards and a touchdown to beat the St. Louis Rams, 20–17. At the time, he was the youngest quarterback to win the big game. Brady was also Super Bowl MVP in 2004.

» Brady was four years old in 1981 when his father took him to the NFC Championship Game. In that game, Joe Montana, Brady's boyhood idol, threw "The Catch" to Dwight Clarke that sent the San Francisco 49ers to the Super Bowl.

HEIGHT: 6'4"

WEIGHT: 225 lbs.

BIRTH DATE: 8/3/1977

BIRTHPLACE: San Mateo, California

OM BRADY

FREAKY GOOD

Tim Lincecum is one of the most fearsome pitchers in the game, even if he does look like another Jonas brother. The baby-faced hurler with the funky homemade delivery has dominated National League batters in his short time in the majors. In 2009, the 25-year-old Lincecum, standing 5' 11" and weighing just 170 pounds, led the league in strikeouts, tied for the lead in complete games and shutouts, and won the NL Cy Young Award for the second straight year. There's a reason people call him The Freak.

How can someone so small throw so hard (up to 98 miles per hour) and so deceptively (the movement on his curveball looks like something out of a magic trick)? The secret is the righthander's unique pitching motion. Lincecum takes an extremely long stride with his left foot, almost 7½ feet, and keeps his torso facing third base until the last possible moment. The result is a tremendous amount of rotational power. His arm, as he likes to put it, just "comes along for the ride."

The scary part is that Lincecum is still getting better. In 2009, he added a changeup and it became one of baseball's most effective pitches. He also lowered his walks from 84 in 2008 to 68 in '09. No wonder National League hitters are freaking out about The Freak.

BIG NUMBERS

261
Strikeouts by Lincecum in 2009, the most in the National League. His 2.48 ERA ranked second in the NL.

120
Weight difference, in pounds, between Lincecum and New York Yankees ace CC Sabathia.

491
Career strikeouts notched by Lincecum while at the University of Washington, a Pac-10 record. Lincecum was a two-time Pac-10 Pitcher of the Year and a first-team All-America in 2006.

HE SAID IT

" If I would've listened to all those people who said I was too small, I probably wouldn't be here. I also loved baseball. Other sports, the season would come around and I would say to my dad, 'I don't know if I want to play this year.' But baseball had this grip on me."

BIG
MOMENTS

» On July 27, 2009, Lincecum struck out a career-high 15 batters in a game against the Pittsburgh Pirates.

» After the 2008 season, Lincecum was awarded the National League's Cy Young Award as the best pitcher in the league. He joined Dwight Gooden, Bret Saberhagen, and Fernando Valenzuela, as the only pitchers to receive the award in their first full major league season.

» Lincecum was named the 2003 Gatorade High School Player of the Year. Even at age 18, he already threw 94 miles per hour.

HEIGHT: 5'11"

WEIGHT: 170 lbs.

BIRTH DATE:
6/15/1984

BIRTHPLACE:
Bellevue, Washington

TIM

LINCECUM

DWIGHT HOWARD

MAGIC SHOW

With his Popeye muscles and superhuman athleticism, Orlando Magic center Dwight Howard was built to play basketball. Howard stands 6'11" and has a 37-inch vertical leap. He snags rebounds, stuffs shots, and rattles rims better than any center in the NBA.

In 2004, Howard won the Naismith Prep Award as the country's best high school player and entered the NBA draft. The Orlando Magic made him the Number 1 pick, and it paid off right away. He scored 12 points and had 10 rebounds per game as a 19-year-old rookie, becoming the youngest player in NBA history to average a double-double.

Howard dominates on both ends of the floor. In 2008–09, he became the youngest player ever to win the NBA Defensive Player of the Year Award, after leading the league in rebounds (13.8 per game) and blocks (2.9). His contributions have translated into wins for Orlando. The Magic won the Southeast Division title in 2007–08 and '08–09. In the 2009 playoffs, Howard led Orlando to the NBA Finals for only the second time in franchise history. In just six seasons, the player nicknamed Superman has proven that he is the best center in the NBA.

BIG NUMBERS

5,214
Career rebounds pulled down by Howard through the 2008–09 season. He passed Wilt Chamberlain as the youngest NBA player to reach 5,000 boards.

50
Points out of 50 scored by Howard to win the 2008 Slam Dunk contest. He put on a Superman cape and soared through the air to throw down a power dunk.

231
Blocked shots by Howard in 2008–09. He led the league in both blocks and total rebounds (1,093).

HE SAID IT

"People want to see a mean streak, but that's just not me. My teammates know that I take basketball very seriously, but I'm going to have my fun regardless. I'm going to dance in the huddle, I'm going to joke around with the coaching staff, play around with the fans. That's just me."

BIG MOMENTS

» At the 2008 Olympics, Howard fulfilled a childhood dream and won a gold medal with Team USA. He averaged 10.9 points and 5.8 rebounds per game.

» On November 15, 2005, Howard had 21 points and 20 rebounds against Charlotte to become the youngest 20-20 man in NBA history (19 years, 342 days).

» In the 2009 playoffs, Howard led the Magic to their first NBA Finals appearance in 14 years. He averaged 20.3 points and 15.3 boards per game. The Magic lost the series to the Los Angeles Lakers, four games to one.

HEIGHT: 6'11"

WEIGHT: 265 lbs.

BIRTH DATE: 12/8/1985

BIRTHPLACE: Atlanta, Georgia

DWIGH

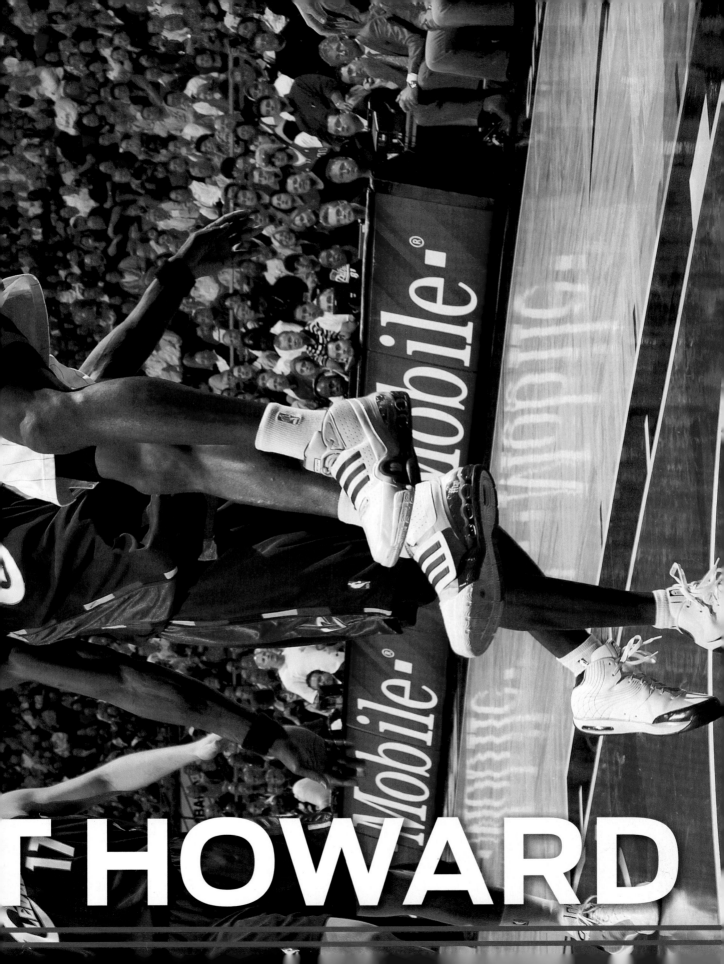

THOWARD

POWER PLAYER

In 2009, Albert Pujols had one of the best seasons of his career. The first baseman hit .327 with 135 RBIs and a major league-high 47 home runs, including five grand slams. Opposing pitchers were so scared of Prince Albert that they walked him 115 times, 44 of which were intentional. So it was no surprise that Pujols was a unanimous choice for National League MVP. (It was the third time he's won the award.) "I think it was the most consistent year," he told reporters. "I was pretty much hot from April until almost September."

Pujols has actually been hot from the minute he arrived in the big leagues. Even when he was bad, he was really good. In 2002, he hit .314 with 34 home runs and 127 RBIs. Those are career numbers for most players. For Pujols, they represent his worst year in the majors.

He hits for average; he hits for power; he hits in the regular season; he hits in the World Series. Pujols is 30 years old and has already accomplished things that no other player has before. In each of his first nine seasons, he's had at least 30 home runs, 100 RBIs, 99 runs, and a .300 batting average. No other player in major league history has started his career with those kinds of stats.

How does he do it? It's all in the swing. It's not the fastest around, but it's short and simple. And Pujols has a knack for putting the fat part of the bat on the ball. When he connects, look out. In a 2009 game, Pujols hit a homer so hard and far that when it hit the BIG MAC LAND sign in leftfield, the ball broke the second letter in BIG. Talk about "I"-popping power.

BIG NUMBERS

49, 50
Home runs and strikeouts, respectively, recorded by Pujols in 2006.

9
Times in his nine-year career that Pujols has finished in the top 10 in the National League in batting average. In 2003, he led the league with a .359 average.

1
Pujols's rank, among active players, in batting average (.334) and slugging percentage (.628).

HE SAID IT

" I don't want to sound cocky or arrogant, but I was always great at this game."

BIG MOMENTS

>> In his first game at Maple Woods Community College in Kansas City, Missouri, Pujols homered and had an unassisted triple play while playing shortstop.

>> In the 2006 playoffs, Pujols led the Cardinals with three home runs and a .439 on-base percentage, helping St. Louis win the World Series.

>> Pujols won MVP awards in 2005, 2008, and 2009. He has never finished outside the top 10 in MVP voting.

HEIGHT: 6'3"

WEIGHT: 230 lbs.

BIRTH DATE: 1/16/1980

BIRTHPLACE: Santo Domingo, Dominican Republic

ALBI

RT PUJOLS

LEADING THE WAY

Before the ball is snapped, Peyton Manning looks more like a turkey trying to line dance than one of the greatest players in football history. He stomps his foot. He flaps his arms. He gestures wildly. But make no mistake: Manning is in complete control.

Manning's pre-snap routine is famous, and nothing shows his talents better. He's a coach on the field. The Indianapolis Colts often run a no-huddle offense, allowing Manning to call plays at the line of the scrimmage. (He knows his options backward and forward. Every week, he studies video for hours and takes page after page of notes.) The strategy helps the Colts keep defenses off-balance. If Manning doesn't like what he sees at the line, he barks out instructions to his teammates and calls an audible, changing the play on the fly.

As elaborate as his pre-snap routine is, what happens when Manning has the ball in his hands is even more impressive. The three-time MVP has a strong arm and is extremely accurate. In 2004 he threw a then-record 49 touchdown passes. He is the Colts' all-time leader in passing yards, completions, and passing touchdowns. With Manning under center, Indianapolis led the NFL in third-down-conversion percentage in the span between 1998 and 2008. That's a sign that the Colts' quarterback has both the smarts to call the right plays and the talent to execute them perfectly. "It's not even close," former Denver Broncos coach Mike Shanahan told SPORTS ILLUSTRATED in 2007. "[Manning is] the best."

BIG NUMBERS

5
Consecutive games in 2004 in which Manning threw four or more touchdown passes, an NFL record.

94.7
Manning's career passing rating through the 2008 season. He leads all active players in that category and ranks second all time to Steve Young (96.8).

3
Associated Press NFL MVP awards won by Manning. Brett Favre is the only other player to have won the award three times.

HE SAID IT

"Once you win, you don't want to quit. You want to win another one. So you have that same hunger, for sure. At least I do."

BIG MOMENTS

>> The Colts selected Manning first overall in the 1998 draft. He set the single-season rookie records for completions (326), passing yards (3,739), and touchdown passes (26).

>> On September 10, 2006, Manning played against his younger brother, Eli, and the New York Giants in a game nicknamed the Manning Bowl. The Colts won the game, 26–21.

>> Manning won his first Super Bowl in 2007, throwing for 247 yards and a touchdown in a 29–17 victory over the Chicago Bears. He was named Super Bowl MVP.

HEIGHT: 6'5"

WEIGHT: 230 lbs.

BIRTH DATE: 3/24/1976

BIRTHPLACE: New Orleans, Louisiana

PEYTO

MANNING

MARCH OF THE PENGUIN

Sidney Crosby has always been advanced for his age. When he was two years old, Crosby started perfecting his slap shot in his basement, which his dad painted like a hockey rink. Crosby used a clothes dryer as a backstop for the goal and blasted so many pucks at the machine that he wrecked it. Crosby's explosive skill would soon be on display on the ice. He starred for youth hockey teams in Canada and won every conceivable award.

By the time he turned 18 and declared for the 2005 NHL draft, Sid the Kid had already been praised by hockey legend Wayne Gretzky and was chosen with the Number 1 pick by the Pittsburgh Penguins.

In his first season in Pittsburgh, Crosby broke Mario Lemieux's rookie records for assists and points. The next season, Crosby won the NHL scoring title (120 points), an amazing accomplishment for someone so young.

He didn't stop there. In 2007–08, Crosby, who was the youngest captain in NHL history, led the Penguins on an exciting playoff run to the Stanley Cup finals. They lost to the Detroit Red Wings in six games, but it didn't take long for Crosby to avenge the defeat. In 2008–09, he came back from a mid-season injury to help Pittsburgh return to the postseason, where it once again faced Detroit in the finals. This time, however, Crosby was not going to be a runner-up. After trailing three games to two, the Penguins rallied and won their first championship in 16 seasons. After the win, Lemieux, now the Penguins' co-owner, said, "When you have Sid, anything is possible."

BIG NUMBERS

120
Points scored by Crosby in 2006–07. The 19-year-old became the first teenager to lead the NHL in scoring since Wayne Gretzky in 1979–80. Crosby finished with 36 goals and 84 assists.

1,713,021
Online votes received by Crosby for the 2009 NHL All-Star Game. It was the highest total any player had ever received.

15
Goals scored by Crosby in the 2008–09 Stanley Cup playoffs. He led the postseason in that category.

HE SAID IT

" I take pride in being a good leader. I try to lead by example on and off the ice."

HEIGHT: 5'11"

WEIGHT: 200 lbs.

BIRTH DATE: 8/7/1987

BIRTHPLACE: Cole Harbour, Nova Scotia, Canada

SIDN

EY CROSBY

REACHING NEW HEIGHTS

LeBron James had perhaps the best season of his career in 2008–09. He won his first MVP award and dominated in ways not seen since Michael Jordan. But James would be the first to call the season a disappointment. Why? Because his team didn't win a championship.

If you want to know why a lot of people think James is this generation's Jordan, just look at how he handles disappointment. The Cavaliers came up short in the Eastern Conference finals, falling to the Orlando Magic in six games. James had been brilliant throughout the playoffs, averaging 35.3 points, 9.1 rebounds, and 7.3 assists per game. But when the buzzer sounded on Cleveland's season, James was furious. You could tell by the way he walked off the floor. "I'm a winner," he explained later. James, like MJ, hates to lose.

But if James keeps putting up huge seasons, he won't be losing much longer. James is a small forward who can pass like a point guard and rebound like a big man, and he does everything for the Cavs. In 2008–09, he became the fourth player in NBA history to lead his team in the five major statistical categories. He scored 28.4 points per game, grabbed 7.6 rebounds, and handed out 7.2 assists. He was masterful on defense, too, making 1.7 steals and 1.1 blocks per game. James developed an amazing talent for running down opponents on breakaways and blocking their layups from behind.

In 2009, James announced that he would give up his number 23 jersey in 2010 to pay tribute to his hero. "I just think what Michael Jordan has done for the game has to be recognized some way soon," James said. Someday they'll be saying the same thing about LeBron.

BIG NUMBERS

30.0
Points per game James averaged in 2007–08 when he won his first NBA scoring title.

24 years, 35 days
James's age when he became the youngest player ever to score 12,000 career points, on February 3, 2009. He ended the 2008–09 season with 12,993.

380
Games it took James to become Cleveland's all-time leading scorer. The previous record holder, Brad Daugherty, needed 548 games.

HE SAID IT

" If I'm just getting my man-strength now, I don't want to see me at 32."

BIG
MOMENTS

》 In the 2006–07 Eastern Conference finals, James led the Cavs to a memorable double-overtime victory against the Detroit Pistons in Game 5. He scored 29 of his team's final 30 points and finished with 48 points total.

》 James scored 14 points and pulled down six boards against Spain to help the United States win the gold medal during the 2008 Olympics.

》 As a senior at St. Vincent-St. Mary High School in Akron, Ohio, James led his team to a 25–1 record and its third state championship in four years. The Irish were named high school national champions by USA Today.

HEIGHT: 6'8"

WEIGHT: 250 lbs.

BIRTH DATE: 12/30/1984

BIRTHPLACE: Akron, Ohio

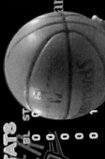

LeB

RON JAMES

MAKING A RUN

Running backs like Adrian Peterson come along about once a generation. An extraordinary blend of speed and power, Peterson runs past most opponents and runs over the rest.

With 4.40-second speed in the 40-yard dash, a 38-inch vertical leap, and a natural ability to find running room, Peterson makes impossible plays look routine. He can fake out multiple tacklers in the backfield, stiff-arm several more, and ramble for 50 yards down the sideline. Then he can do it again.

At the University of Oklahoma in 2004, Peterson won the Jim Brown Trophy as the nation's best running back and was a Heisman Trophy finalist. And he was only a freshman. Even though his next two seasons were shortened because of injury, Peterson still finished with the third-highest career rushing total in Sooners' history.

He stormed into the pros in 2007 with one of the best rookie years of all time. By the midpoint of the season, he'd already had two 200-yard games, a feat never before accomplished by a first-year player. His season ended with a trip to Hawaii for the Pro Bowl, where he was named MVP.

In 2008, he made his second All-Pro team after leading the NFL in rushing with 1,760 yards (a Vikings single-season record). If there's any doubt as to where Peterson's career is headed, consider this: The only other running backs to lead the league in yards per game over their first two seasons are Eric Dickerson, Jim Brown, and Earl Campbell — all Pro Football Hall of Famers.

BIG NUMBERS

296

Yards Peterson ran for in a 2007 game against the San Diego Chargers to break the NFL's all-time single-game rushing record.

60

Yards gained on Peterson's first reception as a pro. The play resulted in a touchdown.

4

Peterson's rank in NFL history for number of rushing yards totaled in a player's first two seasons (3,101).

HE SAID IT

"I want people to remember me as the best player to ever play the game. When you think about football, I want my name to pop in your head."

BIG
MOMENTS

» After rushing for 129 yards and two touchdowns, Peterson was named MVP of the Pro Bowl in just his first NFL season. The only other rookie to win the award is Marshall Faulk.

» Peterson ran away with the 2007 NFL Offensive Rookie of the Year award and set the league record for most yards gained through the first eight games of a career with 1,036.

» As a freshman at Oklahoma, Peterson rushed for 1,925 yards, breaking the Sooners' single-season record. It had been held by Billy Sims.

HEIGHT: 6'1"

WEIGHT: 217 lbs.

BIRTH DATE: 3/21/1985

BIRTHPLACE: Palestine, Texas

ADRIAN

PETERSON

SECOND TO NONE

In the fall of 2009, the rest of the country finally had to acknowledge what Philadelphia Phillies fans had been saying for years: Chase Utley is the best second baseman in the game. He tied a record set by Hall of Famer Reggie Jackson — that's Mr. October — with five home runs in a World Series. And even though his Phillies lost the series to the New York Yankees in six games, many thought Utley should've earned the Series MVP award.

The recognition is well-deserved. In 2009, Utley had another brilliant regular season that went largely unnoticed. He mashed 31 home runs, stole a career-high 23 bases, and played excellent defense at second. While his more famous teammates, such as shortstop Jimmy Rollins and first baseman Ryan Howard — both former National League MVPs — receive most of the attention, it was the publicity-shy Utley who led the Phillies to their second consecutive World Series appearance. "He's one of the most prepared, one of the most dedicated," said Phillies manager Charlie Manuel. "He has the most desire and passion to play the game that I've ever been around."

Utley's performance in the World Series even wowed Reggie Jackson, who seemed a little nervous about the record he now shares with Utley. When asked what he would say to Utley if he ever met him, Jackson replied, "You're good. Now stop." Unfortunately for Jackson, that's unlikely to happen.

BIG NUMBERS

26
Consecutive postseason games in which Utley had successfully reached base, a major league record.

24
Times Utley was hit by a pitch in 2009, the most in baseball. He has led the National League in that category three times.

0
Times Utley was caught stealing in 2009. He finished the season with 23 stolen bases.

HE SAID IT

"The harder you play this game, the more you get out of it. I never want to look in a mirror and say, 'What if?' What if I had run harder? What if I had dived for that ground ball?"

BIG
MOMENTS

» In Game 5 of the 2008 World Series against the Tampa Bay Rays, Utley chased down a ground ball up the middle and faked a throw to first base before firing to home plate so Jason Bartlett could be tagged out. Fans voted the play the 2008 Postseason Moment of the Year.

» In 2006, Chase Utley hit safely in 35 straight games. It was the fourth-longest streak in National League history since 2000.

» Utley hit a grand slam in his first major league game as a starter, on April 24, 2003.

HEIGHT: 6'1"

WEIGHT: 190 lbs.

BIRTH DATE: 12/17/1978

BIRTHPLACE: Pasadena, California

CH

ASE UTLEY

PASSING FANCY

Few quarterbacks have inspired a team like Drew Brees has the New Orleans Saints. After going 3–13 in 2005, the Saints plucked Brees out of free agency. The next season, he marched the team to its first NFC Championship Game appearance.

The sudden turnaround was a surprise to everyone except Brees. After a standout college career at Purdue, where he was a two-time Heisman finalist, Brees was drafted by the San Diego Chargers in 2001. He didn't have a great pro start and was benched in 2003. But the precise passer never gave up. He roared back the following season, guiding the Chargers into the playoffs. Brees went on to win the Associated Press Comeback Player of the Year award and make the Pro Bowl. Still, the Chargers cut him loose after 2005. Their loss was New Orleans's gain.

Since 2006, Brees has led all NFL quarterbacks in passing yards. In 2008, he threw for a remarkable 5,069 yards, becoming only the second player in history to break the 5,000-yard mark in a season. Brees made the Saints the hottest team in the league in 2009. One of the highlights of the regular season was a brilliant 38–17 win over the New England Patriots in Week 12. In that game, Brees completed 18 of 23 passes for 371 yards and five touchdowns and had a perfect passer rating.

Brees is among the hardest-working and smartest players in the NFL. His success is well-deserved. "Drew doesn't just show up and expect to play well because he's talented," says Saints safety Darren Sharper. "He prepares himself every day to go out there on Sundays and play at a high level."

BIG NUMBERS

6

Touchdown passes thrown by Brees in Week 1 of the 2009 season, an NFL record for the opening weekend. The Saints beat the Detroit Lions, 45–27.

1

Brees's rank in 2008 for attempts (635), completions (413), passing yards (5,069), and touchdowns (34).

440

Completions made by Brees in 2007, breaking former Oakland Raiders quarterback Rich Gannon's single-season record of 418.

HE SAID IT

" I always evaluate myself in the off-season. I focus on what it's going to take for me to become a better player and better leader."

BIG MOMENTS

» While at Purdue, Brees won the Maxwell Award, given to the nation's most outstanding college football player. He is the Big Ten's all-time leader in passing yards (11,792), touchdown passes (90), and completions (1,026).

» Brees ended the 2008 season with 5,069 passing yards. He was just 16 yards shy of breaking the single-season record held by former Miami Dolphins QB Dan Marino.

» Brees was a co-winner of the 2006 Walter Payton Man of the Year award for his community service. He works with kids through his Brees Dream Foundation and is also a spokesperson for the NFL's Play 60 program that encourages kids to be active for at least 60 minutes a day.

HEIGHT: 6'0"

WEIGHT: 209 lbs.

BIRTH DATE:
1/15/1979

BIRTHPLACE:
Austin, Texas

D

EW BREES

KING OF THE HILLS

Even though his face is usually completely covered, it's easy to spot Shaun White on a mountain. Just look for the guy catching bigger air than anyone else. With a wild mane of red hair that has earned him the nickname the Flying Tomato, White is the most recognizable snowboarder in the world.

He's also one of the most dominant athletes to ever strap into a board. He has won 14 career medals, including nine gold, at the Winter X Games. In 2009, he took home golds in superpipe and slopestyle. He was also the Male Athlete of the Year in snowboarding at the 2008–09 Winter Dew Tour and won three straight halfpipe titles at the U.S. Open Snowboarding Championships from 2006 through '08.

But White's biggest accomplishment came in 2006, when he won the gold medal in halfpipe snowboarding at the Winter Olympics in Torino, Italy. He joked about hanging the prize from the rearview mirror in his car. (He now owns a Lamborghini.) But it was obvious how much the victory truly meant to him when the U.S. flag was raised during the medal ceremony and White teared up.

In the warmer months, White trades in his snowboard for a skateboard. He has three X Games medals in vert skateboarding, as well as three Dew Tour gold medals in the event. With so many achievements, it's easy to forget that White is still only 23 years old. Expect him to be a major force in snowboarding and skateboarding for many years to come.

BIG NUMBERS

17
Number of X Games medals won by White. Fourteen are for snowboarding and three for vert skateboarding.

46.8
White's winning halfpipe score (out of 50) in the finals of the 2006 Winter Olympics in Torino, Italy.

1260
The degrees of rotation (three-and-a-half complete spins) on tough tricks White had been practicing for the 2010 Vancouver Olympics.

HE SAID IT

" I'm excited to go back to the Olympics. It brings motivation for me to learn new tricks and to do better things and to stay healthy."

BIG
MOMENTS

» In the 2006 Olympics, White barely qualified for the finals. Then he dropped into the pipe, hit back-to-back 1080s and made history.

» When he was five, White had surgery on his heart to repair a birth defect. A year later, he hopped on a snowboard for the first time and started landing jumps right away.

» At the 2007 U.S. Open, White returned from injury to successfully defend his national title and was named the first Burton Global Open Champion.

HEIGHT: 5'8"

WEIGHT: 139 lbs.

BIRTH DATE:
9/3/1986

BIRTHPLACE:
Carlsbad,
California

SH

UN WHITE

BIG STARS TRIVIA

1. LeBron James *(above)* says he'll switch to a number 6 jersey for the 2010—11 season. Which NBA great did *not* wear number 6?
A. Julius Erving
B. Bill Russell
C. Wilt Chamberlain

2. In 2007, Adrian Peterson set the NFL single-game rushing mark (296 yards). Whose record did he break?
A. Shaun Alexander
B. Jamal Lewis
C. LaDainian Tomlinson

3. Through 2009, Albert Pujols led active players with a .334 career batting average. Who is the all-time leader with a .366 average?
A. Ted Williams
B. Pete Rose
C. Ty Cobb

4. What year did halfpipe snowboarding make its debut as a Winter Olympic sport?
A. 1998
B. 2002
C. 2006

5. Who was drafted number 2 behind Peyton Manning *(below)* **in 1998?**
A. Ryan Leaf
B. Deion Branch
C. Tree Rollins

6. In 2008, the NHL held the first Winter Classic outdoor game at Ralph Wilson Stadium *(above)* **between the Pittsburgh Penguins and the Buffalo Sabres. Which stadium has *not* hosted the event?**
A. Yankee Stadium
B. Wrigley Field
C. Fenway Park

7. Tim Lincecum *(above)* **won the NL Cy Young Award in 2008 and '09. Who was the last pitcher to win the award two years in a row?**
A. Pedro Martinez
B. Randy Johnson
C. Johan Santana

8. What university did Chase Utley go to?
A. Harvard
B. UCLA
C. LSU

9. Which superhero did Dwight Howard dress up as in the 2008 Slam Dunk Contest?
A. Batman
B. Spider-Man
C. Superman

10. Which athlete attended the same high school as Barry Bonds (Junipero Serra High in San Mateo, California)?
A. Shaun White
B. Tiger Woods
C. Tom Brady

11. In 2008, Drew Brees nearly broke the single-season record for passing yards held by Dan Marino *(below)*. **Who is the career leader in that category?**
A. Brett Favre
B. Dan Marino
C. Fran Tarkenton

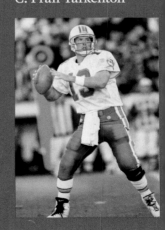

Answers: 1. C, 2. B, 3. C, 4. A, 5. A, 6. A, 7. B, 8. B, 9. C, 10. C, 11. A